A-B-A-B-A—
a Book of
Pattern Play

To Emma
—B.P.C.

Pattern:
A repeating
arrangement of
numbers, colors,
shapes, or other
items

A-B-A-B-A

a Book of Pattern Play

by Brian P. Cleary

illustrated by Brian Gable

Ⓜ MILLBROOK PRESS / MINNEAPOLIS

A pattern shows repeating
in a certain type of Way

that helps you so
you know what's next,

It's sort of an arrangement of colors,

shapes,

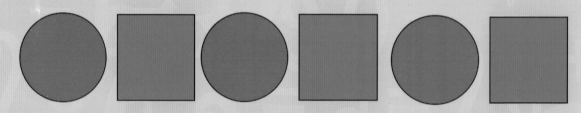

or things,

in a way that is predictable,
as in this row of rings.

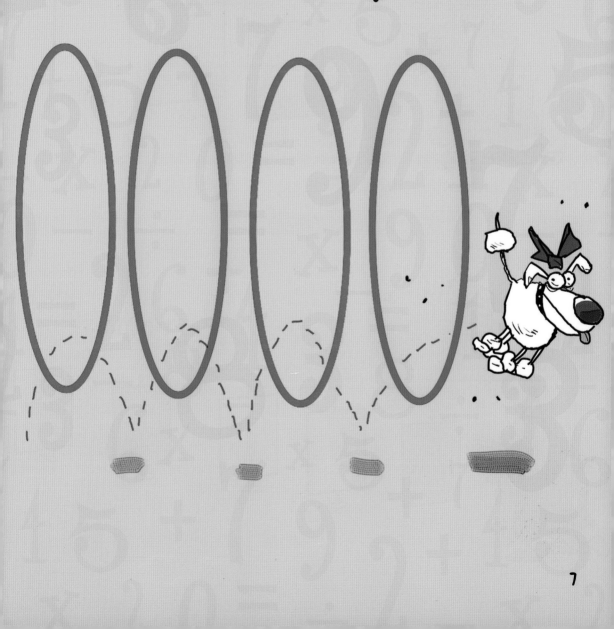

See the colors? Green, red, gold,

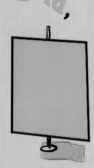

then green, red, gold, green, red.

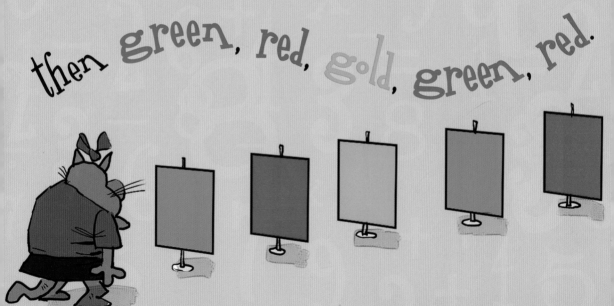

8

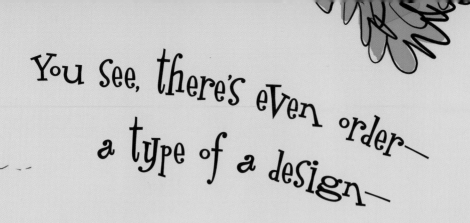

You see, there's even order—
a type of a design—

that's found among the children
who are waiting here in line.

First a girl and then a boy,

then girl,

then boy,

and then—

the **pattern** just continues here
until you reach the end.

The pattern on this kitchen floor
is white,
then black,
then white.

If this design is followed, then the floor will turn out right.

Patterns also can be found in numbers—take a look:

A pattern shows repeating in a certain type of way

like A, B, A, B, A...

...helps you so ...ou know what's next.

each page, the number grows by one
as you read through this book.

17

1, 2, 3 and 1, 2, 3 . . .

You see a **pattern** here?

It goes from 1 to 2, then 3-
it's all becoming clear!

See these numbers? 2, 4, 6,
then 8, 10, 12, 14 . . .

Try to guess which number's next just based on what you've seen.

21

The pattern has us count by 2s, so it would follow then

2, 4, 6,
8, 10,
12, 14,
___

+2

that 16 would be next in line.
Shall we try once again?

Start with 1, then 3, then 5, and follow that with 7.

The number 9 is what comes next.
Then—you guessed right—11.

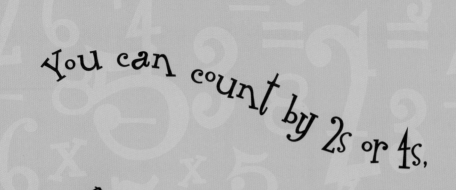

You can count by 2s or 4s,

by 5s or 10s or 20s.

Patterns are found everywhere—

in cards,

on yards,

on a dress.

And knowing them will help you start a **pattern** of success!

So, what is a **pattern**?
Do you know?

30

Find activities, games, and more at
www.brianpcleary.com

ABOUT THE AUTHOR & ILLUSTRATOR

BRIAN P. CLEARY is the author of the best-selling Words Are CATegorical® series as well as the Math Is CATegorical©, Food Is CATegorical™, Adventures in Memory™, and Sounds Like Reading® series. He has also written The Punctuation Station, The Laugh Stand: Adventures in Humor, and several other books. He lives in Cleveland, Ohio.

BRIAN GABLE is the illustrator of many Words Are CATegorical® books and the Math Is CATegorical® series. Mr. Gable also works as a political cartoonist for the Globe and Mail newspaper in Toronto, Canada.

Text copyright © 2010 by Brian P. Cleary
Illustrations copyright © 2010 by Lerner Publishing Group, Inc.

Millbrook Press
A division of Lerner Publishing Group, Inc.
241 First Avenue North
Minneapolis, MN 55401 U.S.A.

Website address: www.lernerbooks.com

Library of Congress Cataloging-in-Publication Data

Cleary, Brian P., 1959—
    A-B-A-B-A—a book of pattern play / by Brian P. Cleary ; illustrated by Brian Gable.
        p.   cm. — (Math is categorical)
    ISBN: 978—0—8225—7880—2 (lib. bdg. : alk. paper)
    1. Pattern perception—Juvenile literature. 2. Categories (Mathematics)—Juvenile literature. I. Gable,
    Brian, 1949— ill. II. Title.
    Q327.C54 2010
    003'.52—dc22   2009049386

Manufactured in the United States of America
1 — DP — 7/15/2010